Flak

by Iain Gray

Lang**Syne**

PUBLISHING

WRITING *to* REMEMBER

Lang**Syne**

PUBLISHING

WRITING *to* REMEMBER

79 Main Street, Newtongrange,
Midlothian EH22 4NA
Tel: 0131 344 0414   Fax: 0845 075 6085
E-mail: info@lang-syne.co.uk
www.langsyneshop.co.uk

Design by Dorothy Meikle
Printed by Printwell Ltd
© Lang Syne Publishers Ltd 2016

ISBN 978-1-85217-317-3

Flaherty

MOTTO:
Fortune favours the bold
(or) Fortune favoured.

CREST:
A lizard atop a helmet.

NAME variations include:
Ó Flaithbheartaigh (*Gaelic*)
O'Flagerty
O'Flaherty
Faherty
Fairty
Feherty
Flaverty
Fleharty
Fluharty
Lafferty
Laverty

Chapter one:
Origins of Irish surnames

**According to an old saying, there are two types of Irish –
those who actually are Irish and those who wish they were.**

This sentiment is only one example of the allure that the
high romance and drama of the proud nation's history holds
for thousands of people scattered across the world today.

It's a sad fact, however, that the vast majority of Irish
surnames are found far beyond Irish shores, rather than on
the Emerald Isle itself.

The population stood at around eight million souls in
1841, but today it stands at fewer than six million.

This is mainly a tragic consequence of the potato
famine, also known as the Great Hunger, which devastated
Ireland between 1845 and 1849.

The Irish peasantry had become almost wholly reliant
for basic sustenance on the potato, first introduced from the
Americas in the seventeenth century.

When the crop was hit by a blight, at least 800,000
people starved to death while an estimated two million
others were forced to seek a new life far from their native
shores – particularly in America, Canada, and Australia.

The effects of the potato blight continued until about
1851, by which time a firm pattern of emigration had
become established.

Ireland's loss, however, was to the gain of the countries in which the immigrants settled, contributing enormously, as their descendants do today, to the well being of the nations in which their forefathers settled.

But those who were forced through dire circumstance to establish a new life in foreign parts never forgot their roots, or the proud heritage and traditions of the land that gave them birth.

Nor do their descendants.

It is a heritage that is inextricably bound up in the colourful variety of Irish names themselves – and the origin and history of these names forms an integral part of the vibrant drama that is the nation's history, one of both glorious fortune and tragic misfortune.

This history is well documented, and one of the most important and fascinating of the earliest sources are *The Annals of the Four Masters*, compiled between 1632 and 1636 by four friars at the Franciscan Monastery in County Donegal.

Compiled from earlier sources, and purporting to go back to the Biblical Deluge, much of the material takes in the mythological origins and history of Ireland and the Irish.

This includes tales of successive waves of invaders and settlers such as the Fomorians, the Partholonians, the Nemedians, the Fir Bolgs, the Tuatha De Danann, and the Laigain.

Of particular interest are the *Milesian Genealogies*,

because the majority of Irish clans today claim a descent from either Heremon, Ir, or Heber – three of the sons of Milesius, a king of what is now modern day Spain.

These sons invaded Ireland in the second millennium B.C, apparently in fulfilment of a mysterious prophecy received by their father.

This Milesian lineage is said to have ruled Ireland for nearly 3,000 years, until the island came under the sway of England's King Henry II in 1171 following what is known as the Cambro-Norman invasion.

This is an important date not only in Irish history in general, but for the effect the invasion subsequently had for Irish surnames.

'Cambro' comes from the Welsh, and 'Cambro-Norman' describes those Welsh knights of Norman origin who invaded Ireland.

But they were invaders who stayed, inter-marrying with the native Irish population and founding their own proud dynasties that bore Cambro-Norman names such as Archer, Barbour, Brannagh, Fitzgerald, Fitzgibbon, Fleming, Joyce, Plunkett, and Walsh – to name only a few.

These 'Cambro-Norman' surnames that still flourish throughout the world today form one of the three main categories in which Irish names can be placed – those of Gaelic-Irish, Cambro-Norman, and Anglo-Irish.

Previous to the Cambro-Norman invasion of the twelfth century, and throughout the earlier invasions and settlement of those wild bands of sea rovers known as the Vikings in the eighth and ninth centuries, the population of the island was relatively small, and it was normal for a person to be identified through the use of only a forename.

But as population gradually increased and there were many more people with the same forename, surnames were adopted to distinguish one person, or one community, from another.

Individuals identified themselves with their own particular tribe, or 'tuath', and this tribe – that also became known as a clann, or clan – took its name from some distinguished ancestor who had founded the clan.

The Gaelic-Irish form of the name Kelly, for example, is Ó Ceallaigh, or O'Kelly, indicating descent from an original 'Ceallaigh', with the 'O' denoting 'grandson of.' The name was later anglicised to Kelly.

The prefix 'Mac' or 'Mc', meanwhile, as with the clans of the Scottish Highlands, denotes 'son of.'

Although the Irish clans had much in common with their Scottish counterparts, one important difference lies in what are known as 'septs', or branches, of the clan.

Septs of Scottish clans were groups who often bore an entirely different name from the clan name but were under the clan's protection.

In Ireland, septs were groups that shared the same name and who could be found scattered throughout the four provinces of Ulster, Leinster, Munster, and Connacht.

The 'golden age' of the Gaelic-Irish clans, infused as their veins were with the blood of Celts, pre-dates the Viking invasions of the eighth and ninth centuries and the Norman invasion of the twelfth century, and the sacred heart of the country was the Hill of Tara, near the River Boyne, in County Meath.

Known in Gaelic as 'Teamhar na Rí', or Hill of Kings, it was the royal seat of the 'Ard Rí Éireann', or High King of Ireland, to whom the petty kings, or chieftains, from the island's provinces were ultimately subordinate.

It was on the Hill of Tara, beside a stone pillar known as the Irish 'Lia Fáil', or Stone of Destiny, that the High Kings were inaugurated and, according to legend, this stone would emit a piercing screech that could be heard all over Ireland when touched by the hand of the rightful king.

The Hill of Tara is today one of the island's main tourist attractions.

Opposition to English rule over Ireland, established in the wake of the Cambro-Norman invasion, broke out frequently and the harsh solution adopted by the powerful forces of the Crown was to forcibly evict the native Irish from their lands.

These lands were then granted to Protestant colonists, or 'planters', from Britain.

Many of these colonists, ironically, came from Scotland and were the descendants of the original 'Scotti', or 'Scots', who gave their name to Scotland after migrating there in the fifth century A.D., from the north of Ireland.

Colonisation entailed harsh penal laws being imposed on the majority of the native Irish population, stripping them practically of all of their rights.

The Crown's main bastion in Ireland was Dublin and its environs, known as the Pale, and it was the dispossessed peasantry who lived outside this Pale, desperately striving to eke out a meagre living.

It was this that gave rise to the modern-day expression of someone or something being 'beyond the pale'.

Attempts were made to stamp out all aspects of the ancient Gaelic-Irish culture, to the extent that even to bear a Gaelic-Irish name was to invite discrimination.

This is why many Gaelic-Irish names were anglicised with, for example, and noted above, Ó Ceallaigh, or O'Kelly, being anglicised to Kelly.

Succeeding centuries have seen strong revivals of Gaelic-Irish consciousness, however, and this has led to many families reverting back to the original form of their name, while the language itself is frequently found on the fluent tongues of an estimated 90,000 to 145,000 of the island's population.

Ireland's turbulent history of religious and political strife is one that lasted well into the twentieth century, a landmark century that saw the partition of the island into the twenty-six counties of the independent Republic of

Ireland, or Eire, and the six counties of Northern Ireland, or Ulster.

Dublin, originally founded by Vikings, is now a vibrant and truly cosmopolitan city while the proud city of Belfast is one of the jewels in the crown of Ulster.

It was Saint Patrick who first brought the light of Christianity to Ireland in the fifth century A.D.

Interpretations of this Christian message have varied over the centuries, often leading to bitter sectarian conflict – but the many intricately sculpted Celtic Crosses found all over the island are symbolic of a unity that crosses the sectarian divide.

It is an image that fuses the 'old gods' of the Celts with Christianity.

All the signs from the early years of this new millennium indicate that sectarian strife may soon become a thing of the past – with the Irish and their many kinsfolk across the world, be they Protestant or Catholic, finding common purpose in the rich tapestry of their shared heritage.

Chapter two:

Of the sword

**'Fortune favours the bold' is the particularly apt motto
of the proud clan of Flaherty, noted from earliest times
as ferocious in war and defiant in defence of their
ancient rights and privileges.**

The Gaelic form of the name is Ó Flaithbheartaigh,
indicating 'bright ruler', and it was these 'bright rulers' who
dominated the western section of Connacht, which, along
with Ulster, Leinster and Munster is one of Ireland's four
provinces.

The family name comes from a tenth century Connacht
prince known as Flaithbhertach who, in turn, was a son of
the Rí Iarthair Connacht, or Lord of West Connacht.

Their main seat was an area near present day Moycullen
in Co. Galway, while they were also in possession of the
Aran Islands, off the west coast of Ireland.

In Ulster, meanwhile, the form of the name became
'Laverty', or 'Lafferty', and this sept of the Flahertys
flourished in an area of Co. Donegal, with their chief known
as the Lord of Aileach.

The Flaherty pedigree is truly illustrious, with bearers of
the name claimants to a proud descent from Conn
Céthchathach, the Gaelic form for Conn of the Hundred
Battles.

Ard Rí, or High King of Ireland from about 177 to 212 A.D., this ancestor of the Flahertys of today figures prominently in what are known as the *Fenian Cycle* of tales, also known as the *Ossianic Cycle* and thought to date from the third century.

One of Conn's ancestors is said to have been no less than Goidel Glas, who is reputed to have created the Gaelic-Irish language after he combined and refined the 72 known languages of his time.

The result is the language of poets that thrills like the plucked strings of an Irish harp throughout the *Fenian Cycle*.

As a youth, Conn is said to have met two mysterious figures who predicted he and his descendants would rule Ireland.

The strange figures who are reputed by legend to have appeared to him, enshrouded in mist, were a beautiful young maiden known as Sovranty who, wearing a golden crown and seated on a crystal chair, was accompanied by the sun god Lugh, patron of arts and crafts.

It is said they prophesied his descendants would rule until the death of the old Gods – which in fact did occur in the form of St. Patrick and the new religious pantheon of Christianity.

Conn attained the High Kingship after overthrowing Cathair Mór, also known as Mal, who had killed his father.

But his kingship was never secure because he had to

fight a relentless succession of battles with his great rival Eogan Mór, also known as Mug Nadhat, king of the Dál nAraide, or Cruithe, who occupied the northeastern territories of Ireland.

It was because of the number of battles Conn fought with these Cruithne, or Picts, that he earned the title of Conn Céthchathach – Conn of the Hundred Battles.

The two rival kings achieved a temporary accommodation after the island was divided between themselves, the division starting at a ridge known as Eiscir Riada, which traverses the island from Galway Bay to Dublin.

Mug's territory in the south was known as Leth Moga Nuadht, while Conn's northern territory was known as Leth Cuinn.

But it was not long before the ambitious and fiercely proud warriors were again locked in battle.

Mug gained the upper hand for a time after storing up grain in his territories after taking heed of a dire Druidic prophecy of famine – but Conn eventually defeated his rival, taking him by surprise in a night raid near present-day Tullamore, in Co. Offaly.

Conn consolidated his kingship over Ireland, but his success was short-lived, destined to die under the glinting blades of fifty warriors who had managed to breach the defences of his royal bastion of Tara after disguising themselves as women.

At the head of these warriors was the vengeful Tibride

Tirech, son of the Cathair Mór whom Conn had killed years earlier in revenge for the death of his own father.

The Flahertys were also members of the confederation of clans known as the Uí Briuin, indicating a descent from Brian, a son of Niall Noíghiallach, better known to posterity as the great late fourth century warrior king Niall of the Nine Hostages.

Duach Galach, one of Brian's sons, is recognised as having been 'the first Christian ancestor' of the Flahertys, with legend holding that he extended hospitality to St. Patrick when the saint travelled through Connacht on his early fourth century Christian mission to Ireland.

The saint, who predicted that Duach would reign one day as King of Connacht, later attended his inauguration.

The Uí Briuin split into three septs – the Uí Briuin Ai, Uí Briuin Bréifne and the Uí Briuin Seola.

It was the Flahertys who were of the Uí Briuin Seola, and one of their main strongholds was a heavily fortified crannog, or small island, in the middle of Lough Hackett.

Renowned and feared for their prowess in battle, Flaherty chieftains were known as 'O'Flaherty of the Sword', with the chieftain Eamon Laidir, or Strong Edward, reputed to have been able to cleave his way through the massed ranks of his foes.

Enemies there were aplenty – with the Flahertys among the native Irish clans who were frequently at war with one another in disputes over slighted honour or territory.

The Flaherty crest features a lizard, or eft, and the colourful legend behind its origins concerns the clan chief Amhalgaidh Earchoraigh, or Awley of the Eft.

Closely pursued by enemies, he is said to have collapsed exhausted inside a cave and fallen into a deep sleep.

It was thanks to a small lizard crawling over his face and neck that he managed to wake up in time to flee the cave and evade his pursuers.

Noted seafarers, the Flahertys served as admirals of the fleet to the Royal House of the O'Connors of Connacht – but not all of their seafaring activities were in the service of the O'Connors.

Along with the neighbouring clan of O'Malley, they frequently engaged in piracy, exacting tribute at the point of a blade from vessels sailing to and from the bustling port served by Galway City.

The two clans forged a particularly close bond in the mid-sixteenth century when Donal O'Flaherty, chieftain of his clan, married Grace O'Malley, daughter of the O'Malley chieftain Owen O'Malley.

Known as The Sea Queen of Connacht, or The Pirate Queen of Connacht, she was only a young girl when she first went to sea with her father.

Soon proving herself the equal of her male seafaring kin, she captained O'Malley ships and, later, Flaherty vessels as they intercepted trading vessels.

Any resistance was met with violence and the

O'Malleys and Flahertys became so feared by the good citizens of Galway City that a sign stating 'From the ferocious O'Flahertys may God protect us' is said to have hung over one of the city gates.

But the family have somewhat redeemed themselves since the grim times of piracy on the high seas – with a number of bearers of the name having served in recent years in the honoured and trusted position of Mayors of Galway City.

What proved to be the death knell of the ancient way of life of native Irish clans such as the Flahertys was sounded in the late twelfth century.

This was in the form of the Norman invasion of the island and the subsequent consolidation of the power of the English Crown.

English dominion over Ireland was ratified through the Treaty of Windsor of 1175, under the terms of which the O'Connor chieftain Rory O'Connor, for example, was allowed to rule territory unoccupied by the Normans only in the role of a vassal of the English monarch.

It proved to be a highly volatile recipe for disaster, as in succeeding centuries the island was frequently torn apart in a series of bloody rebellions against English rule and the increasing encroachment on the territories held by the native Irish.

Chapter three:

Rebellion and massacre

It had been nearly 100 years before the late twelfth century Norman invasion of Ireland that Flaherty O'Flaherty had wrested control of the province of Connacht from the O'Connors.

But six years later, shortly before he was killed in battle, he took the decision to hand back the kingship of the province to the more powerful O'Connors.

By 1225, in the aftermath of the Norman invasion, the fortunes of the Flahertys and the O'Connors were closely bound together as both clans battled against waves of Anglo-Norman settlers.

Much of the Flaherty territory in Connacht was seized by a combination of force of arms and subterfuge by the Anglo-Norman settlers known as de Burgh, or Burke, and the clan was forced into the humiliating position of having to pay them rent for those lands they still held.

One of the Burkes was despatched to the Flaherty stronghold of Aughanure Castle, in Oughterard, to collect rent that was due.

The Flahertys were enjoying a magnificent banquet at the time, and invited the unsuspecting Burke to join them.

He had no sooner tucked into the feast than a concealed

flagstone under his chair was pressed and he was sent tumbling into the river below.

Retrieving his body from the river, the Flahertys cut off his head and, placing it in a sack, sent it back to the Burkes as 'O'Flaherty's Rent.'

Violence was merely met by even more violence as the battle-lines were drawn between the native Gaelic-Irish and increasing waves of Anglo-Norman settlers.

One indication of the harsh treatment meted out to the native Irish can be found in a desperate plea sent to Pope John XII by Roderick O'Carroll of Ely, Donald O'Neill of Ulster, and a number of other Irish chieftains in 1318.

They stated: 'As it very constantly happens, whenever an Englishman, by perfidy or craft, kills an Irishman, however noble, or however innocent, be he clergy or layman, there is no penalty or correction enforced against the person who may be guilty of such wicked murder.

'But rather the more eminent the person killed and the higher rank which he holds among his own people, so much more is the murderer honoured and rewarded by the English, and not merely by the people at large, but also by the religious and bishops of the English race.'

The plight of clans such as the Flahertys became even worse because of a policy of 'plantation', or settlement of loyal Protestants on their ancient lands.

This started during the reign from 1491 to 1547 of Henry VIII, whose Reformation effectively outlawed the established Roman Catholic faith throughout his dominions, and continued throughout the subsequent reigns of Elizabeth I, James I (James VI of Scotland), and in the wake of the Cromwellian invasion of 1649.

In an insurrection that exploded in 1641, at least 2,000 Protestant settlers were massacred at the hands of Catholic landowners and their native Irish peasantry, while thousands more were stripped of their belongings and driven from their lands to seek refuge where they could.

One of the worst excesses against the settlers occurred in February of 1642 and is known to posterity as the Massacre at Shrule – a massacre in which the Flahertys are unfortunately understood to have played a role.

A large number of English settlers, including Dr. John Maxwell, the Protestant bishop of Killala, had surrendered to the rebels at Castlebar on the understanding that they would be allowed to keep their weapons and given safe passage to Galway City.

After being held for a time at Shrule Castle, whose ruins can be seen to this day on the boundaries of Co. Mayo and Co. Galway, the rebel leader Lord Mayo arranged for them to be given an escort towards Galway City.

But shortly after the party departed from Shrule, and unknown to Lord Mayo, the rebel Edmund Burke, who was in charge of the escort, ordered his soldiers to fire on the helpless civilians.

Among these soldiers were a number of Flahertys, who

are estimated to have helped to kill upwards of 65 civilians.

Atrocities such as this served to fuel a burning desire on the part of Protestants for revenge against the rebels.

The English Civil War intervened to prevent immediate action, but following the execution of Charles I in 1649 and the consolidation of the power of England's Oliver Cromwell, the time was ripe.

The Lord Protector, as he was named, descended on Ireland at the head of a 20,000-strong army that landed at Ringford, near Dublin, in August of 1649, and the consequences of this Cromwellian conquest still resonate throughout the island today.

Cromwell had three main aims: to quash all forms of rebellion, to 'remove' all Catholic landowners who had taken part in the rebellion and to convert the native Irish to the Protestant faith.

An early warning of the terrors that were in store for the native Catholic Irish came when the northeastern town of Drogheda was stormed and taken in September and between 2,000 and 4,000 of its inhabitants killed, including priests who were summarily put to the sword.

The defenders of Drogheda's St. Peter's Church, who had refused to surrender, were burned to death as they huddled for refuge in the steeple and the church was deliberately torched.

A similar fate awaited Wexford, on the southeast coast, where at least 1,500 of its inhabitants were slaughtered, including 200 defenceless women, despite their pathetic pleas for mercy.

Cromwell soon held the benighted land in a grip of iron, allowing him to implement what amounted to a policy of ethnic cleansing.

His troopers were given free rein to hunt down and kill priests, while Catholic estates were confiscated.

An estimated 11 million acres of land were confiscated and the dispossessed native Irish herded into Connacht and Co. Clare.

An edict was issued stating that any native Irish found east of the River Shannon after May 1, 1654, faced either summary execution or transportation to the West Indies.

Among the many native Irish who suffered was Roderick O'Flaherty, the last recognised chief of the clan.

Born in 1629, he lost the bulk of his ancestral lands in the wake of the Cromwellian confiscations while the remainder was taken from him through the intricate deceptions of his son's father-in-law – the aptly nicknamed 'Nimble Dick' Martin.

O'Flaherty died in great poverty in 1718, but not before he had already established a well-deserved reputation for himself as one of Ireland's greatest historians and chroniclers of the island's turbulent times.

Chapter four:
On the world stage

Bearers of the Flaherty name, in all its variety of spellings, have achieved fame and distinction in a diverse array of pursuits and callings.

In the world of film, **Robert J. Flaherty** was the pioneering American filmmaker who was born in 1884 at Iron Mountain, Michigan, and who died in 1951.

He was a prospector in the Hudson Bay region of Canada, working for a railroad company, when in 1913 one of his superiors suggested that he should take a motion picture camera along with him on one of his expeditions in order to record the people and wildlife that he encountered.

No one could have foreseen at the time what the outcome would be.

Fascinated by the local Inuit people, Flaherty recorded their everyday lives on film – but the film was destroyed in an accidental fire.

Undaunted, Flaherty started filming again from scratch and the eventual result was the 1922 *Nanook of the North* – the world's first commercially successful feature length documentary film.

Abandoning his career as a prospector for life as a full-time filmmaker, he produced several other acclaimed documentary films, including the 1948 *Louisiana Story*, which received an Academy Award for Best Original Story.

Earlier documentary works included the 1931 *Industrial Britain* and the 1934 *Man of Aran*.

It is in recognition of his status as one of the pioneers of documentary film that the Robert J. Flaherty Award is presented annually by BAFTA for Best One-Off Documentary.

Flaherty's wife and collaborator in the making of many of his films was **Francis H. Flaherty**, who was born in 1884.

It was she who penned the story to accompany the award-winning *Louisiana Story*, while in 1971, a year before her death, she appeared in *Hidden and Seeking*, a feature length documentary on their film work.

In contemporary times, **Joe Flaherty**, born in 1941 in Pittsburgh, Pennsylvania, is the American-Canadian comedian whose career in comedy started in Chicago with the famed City Theater.

Moving to Canada, he became best known for his work from 1976 to 1984 as a comedy impersonator on the sketch show *SCTV*, while films in which he has appeared include the 1981 *Stripes*, the 1987 *Back to the Future Part 2* and the 2004 *Home on the Range*.

In the world of contemporary music, **Stephen Flaherty** is the American composer for musical theatre who was born in 1960.

Working in collaboration with Lynn Aherns, he is best

known for the shows *Once On This Island*, from 1990, and which was nominated for eight Tony Awards, and the 1998 *Ragtime* – nominated for no less than twelve Tony Awards and which won Best Original Score.

Other works include the 2005 *Loving Repeating* and the 2007 *The Glorious Ones*, while Flaherty and Ahern also wrote the soundtrack for the 1997 movie *Anastasia*.

In the highly competitive world of high finance and business, **Stephen O'Flaherty**, born in 1905 in Co. Wexford and who died in 1982, became one of the Republic of Ireland's first industrial millionaires through the importation from Germany and assembly in Ireland of Volkswagen cars, shortly after the end of the Second World War.

In the often cut-throat world of politics, **Peter Flaherty** was the leading American Democrat politician who was born in 1924 in Pittsburgh, Pennsylvania and who served as mayor of the city from 1970 to 1977 and as Deputy U.S. Attorney General from 1977 to 1978, during the administration of President Jimmy Carter.

Across the U.S. border, **Jim Flaherty**, born in 1949 in Montreal is, at the time of writing, Canada's Minister of Finance, having previously served as Minister of Finance for Ontario.

In the world of sport, **Gilly Flaherty** is the English footballer born in 1991 in London and who, at the time of writing, is a defender with England's international women's team.

On the baseball, field **Patrick Flaherty**, born in 1876 in Mansfield, Pennsylvania, was a pitcher for teams that included the Louisville Colonels, Pittsburgh Pirates and Chicago White Sox, while **Martin Flaherty**, born in 1853, was the talented outfielder who played for the Worcester Ruby Legs.

Nicknamed 'Flash', **John Flaherty**, born in 1967 in New City, New York, is the former American Major League Baseball catcher who played for teams that included the New York Yankees, Boston Red Sox, San Diego Padres and Tampa Bay Devil Rays and who is now a popular television baseball pundit.

While some people actively pursue fame and celebrity, others rather more deservedly acquire it in recognition of their selfless devotion to others, often at great potential cost to themselves.

One truly inspiring example of this can be found in the dramatic life and times of **Monsignor Hugh O'Flaherty**, who was born in 1898 in Cahirciveen, Co. Kerry, and is better known to posterity as 'The Pimpernel of the Vatican.'

Posted to Rome in 1922 to complete his theological studies after studying at Killarney seminary, he was ordained as a priest three years later.

Remaining in Rome to work for the Holy See, he later served as a diplomat of the Vatican in Haiti, Egypt, Santa Domingo and Czechoslovakia – receiving the title of Monsignor in 1934.

As darkness descended on Europe during the Second World War, he visited Allied prisoner-of-war camps in Italy and, finding soldiers who had been reported missing in action, reassured their families back home by reporting on their whereabouts through Vatican Radio.

Following the fall of the Italian dictator Benito Mussolini in 1943, thousands of Allied prisoners were released from their camps in Italy – but they still needed help in finding their way home through what was still German-occupied Europe.

This was where Monsignor Flaherty stepped in, setting up an elaborate network that allowed the escape of not only Allied prisoners but also hundreds of Jews who faced deportation to Nazi death camps.

Many of the escapees were hidden in the homes of sympathisers and Roman Catholic convents while O'Flaherty himself was the subject of a number of S.S. assassination attempts whenever he stepped outside the diplomatic safety of the Vatican.

It was also through Monsignor O'Flaherty, and unknown to the Nazis at the time, that Jewish religious services were conducted in Rome's Basilica di San Clemente, then under the diplomatic protection of the Irish Legation to Italy.

It is estimated that O'Flaherty, who had become a master of disguises in the style of the fictional French Revolution character known as the Scarlet Pimpernel, was responsible for helping to save no less than 4,000 Allied soldiers and Jews from the clutches of the Nazis.

Insisting at the end of the war that German prisoners should be treated humanely, he regularly visited the former S.S. Chief of Rome Herbert Kappler in prison – resulting in the former devotee of the atheist Nazi creed converting to Roman Catholicism in 1959.

Following the foundation of the State of Israel in 1949, Monsignor O'Flaherty was named by the new nation as being 'Righteous Among Nations', while a tree is planted in his honour in Yad Veshem, Jerusalem.

Other awards he received after the war included the C.B.E. and the U.S. Medal of Freedom with Silver Palm.

Refusing a pension from Italy, the truly remarkable but unassuming Monsignor O'Flaherty suffered a stroke in 1960 and returned to his home village of Caharciveen to live with his sister.

He died three years later and was buried in Caharciveen, while a grove of trees was later planted in his honour in Killarney National Park.

Gegory Peck also portrayed his life and times in the 1983 film *The Scarlet and the Black*.

In the creative world of literature, **Katherine O'Flaherty** was the American author whose father hailed from Co. Galway and whose mother was of French descent.

Also known by her married name of Kate Chopin, she was born in 1851 in St. Louis, Missouri, and is recognised as having been a forerunner of feminist authors of the 20th century.

A writer from 1889 to 1902 of short stories for both children and adults, her major works include the 1894 *Bayou Folk* and *A Night in Acadie*, first published in 1897.

An inductee of the St. Louis Hall of Fame, she died in 1904.

Also in the world of literature **Liam O'Flaherty**, born in 1896 in the village of Gort na gCapall on Inishmore, one of the Aran Islands off the west coast of Ireland was the short story writer and novelist considered to have been one of the major figures of what is known as the Irish Renaissance.

Joining the Irish Guards regiment of the British Army during the First World War, he suffered from the terrible effects of shell shock throughout the remainder of his life – but this did not prevent him from writing a number of acclaimed works.

One of these was *The Informer*, later adapted for the screen by his cousin, the famed Hollywood director John Ford.

Although the novel, first published ten years before the screen adaptation, won a prestigious James Tate Black Memorial Prize, one of his best works is considered to be his first novel, *Thy Neighbour's Wife*, published in 1923.

Flaherty, who died in 1984, is particularly regarded for having written many of his works in his native Irish.

Key dates in Ireland's history from the first settlers to the formation of the Irish Republic:

circa 7000 B.C. Arrival and settlement of Stone Age people.

circa 3000 B.C. Arrival of settlers of New Stone Age period.

circa 600 B.C. First arrival of the Celts.

200 A.D. Establishment of Hill of Tara, Co. Meath, as seat of the High Kings.

circa 432 A.D. Christian mission of St. Patrick.

800-920 A.D. Invasion and subsequent settlement of Vikings.

1002 A.D. Brian Boru recognised as High King.

1014 Brian Boru killed at battle of Clontarf.

1169-1170 Cambro-Norman invasion of the island.

1171 Henry II claims Ireland for the English Crown.

1366 Statutes of Kilkenny ban marriage between native Irish and English.

1529-1536 England's Henry VIII embarks on religious Reformation.

1536 Earl of Kildare rebels against the Crown.

1541 Henry VIII declared King of Ireland.

1558 Accession to English throne of Elizabeth I.

1565 Battle of Affane.

1569-1573 First Desmond Rebellion.

1579-1583 Second Desmond Rebellion.

1594-1603 Nine Years War.

1606 Plantation' of Scottish and English settlers.

1607	Flight of the Earls.
1632-1636	Annals of the Four Masters compiled.
1641	Rebellion over policy of plantation and other grievances.
1649	Beginning of Cromwellian conquest.
1688	Flight into exile in France of Catholic Stuart monarch James II as Protestant Prince William of Orange invited to take throne of England along with his wife, Mary.
1689	William and Mary enthroned as joint monarchs; siege of Derry.
1690	Jacobite forces of James defeated by William at battle of the Boyne (July) and Dublin taken.
1691	Athlone taken by William; Jacobite defeats follow at Aughrim, Galway, and Limerick; conflict ends with Treaty of Limerick (October) and Irish officers allowed to leave for France.
1695	Penal laws introduced to restrict rights of Catholics; banishment of Catholic clergy.
1704	Laws introduced constricting rights of Catholics in landholding and public office.
1728	Franchise removed from Catholics.
1791	Foundation of United Irishmen republican movement.
1796	French invasion force lands in Bantry Bay.
1798	Defeat of Rising in Wexford and death of United Irishmen leaders Wolfe Tone and Lord Edward Fitzgerald.

1800	Act of Union between England and Ireland.
1803	Dublin Rising under Robert Emmet.
1829	Catholics allowed to sit in Parliament.
1845-1849	The Great Hunger: thousands starve to death as potato crop fails and thousands more emigrate.
1856	Phoenix Society founded.
1858	Irish Republican Brotherhood established.
1873	Foundation of Home Rule League.
1893	Foundation of Gaelic League.
1904	Foundation of Irish Reform Association.
1913	Dublin strikes and lockout.
1916	Easter Rising in Dublin and proclamation of an Irish Republic.
1917	Irish Parliament formed after Sinn Fein election victory.
1919-1921	War between Irish Republican Army and British Army.
1922	Irish Free State founded, while six northern counties remain part of United Kingdom as Northern Ireland, or Ulster; civil war up until 1923 between rival republican groups.
1949	Foundation of Irish Republic after all remaining constitutional links with Britain are severed.